How To
Be Yourself

Easy steps to overcoming insecurities and strengthening your life

Jane Briscoe & Simone Essex

BALBOA.
PRESS

A DIVISION OF HAY HOUSE

Interior Graphics/Art Credit: Katie O'Malley

Edited by Bermingham Books
Design & Typesetting by Katie O'Malley
Author Photo by Dalai Liddy
Cover and Inside Photos by iStockphoto LP
Audio CD Production by Coastlife Digital

Balboa Press books may be ordered through booksellers or by contacting:

Balboa Press
A Division of Hay House
1663 Liberty Drive
Bloomington, IN 47403
www.balboapress.com.au
1-(877) 407-4847

ISBN: 978-1-4525-0405-6 (sc)
ISBN: 978-1-4525-0406-3 (e)

How To
Be Yourself

Jane Briscoe & Simone Essex

Contents

Preface

The very first ideas for this book were scribbled down on a tiny notepad while on a flight back home to the Sunshine Coast in Queensland, Australia. We had attended the world's largest forum on Happiness and Its Causes and were feeling very much alive and liberated, from this fascinating fusion of Western and Eastern science and philosophy.

After listening to an extraordinary faculty of speakers demonstrate how happiness is within reach of us all, our ideas for applying these principles into everyday life were endless. Armed with a diverse collection of tools and techniques for a happier life, we decided to write a book. And not just any book, an easy to read, down to earth book that teaches you how to be yourself and be happy.

While browsing through the conference bookshop we were like kids in a candy store, however we noticed that the best books were largely written in a heavy, academic style that could appear a little daunting to the busy, everyday person. We wanted to put all of these revolutionary therapy models and research findings into our own melting pot and produce a practical, step-by-step guide that has the power to change thinking patterns and even the way people live.

Our first step was to listen to our audience. We wanted to know precisely what people believed held them back. To do this we set up a simple website with an online survey and asked our audience to describe the one thing that stopped them from being themselves. In exchange for their time respondents were given a free copy of the *How To Be Yourself* eBook once it was complete. We anticipated about 20 to 30 responses but to our astonishment, we received 590 responses from people from all corners of the globe.

What we learnt was invaluable. Not only was this longing to 'be yourself' cross-cultural, the dominant, underlying theme in all responses was the same. It was the fear of what others think that holds us back. With this in mind we set about writing a book to teach people about how the human mind works, why we tend to worry about what others think and how to overcome these unhelpful thinking patterns.

But who are we to give you guidance? Why should you trust what is written on these pages? Unlike many self-help books available these days, *How To be Yourself* has been co-written by a professional psychologist. Jane Briscoe has been a registered psychologist since 1980 and practices clinical and counselling psychology and hypnotherapy on the Sunshine Coast, Queensland, Australia.

While Jane finds her private practice exciting and rewarding, she realises the people who actually walk through her door are just the tip of the iceberg of those she can help. There are hundreds of thousands of people out there who are yearning to live a happier life but have no idea where to start. By writing this book we aim to help more people to stop struggling with unnecessary worry and start to really live.

The core principals you will learn in *How To Be Yourself* come from components of acceptance and commitment therapy (ACT), positive psychology, hypnotherapy, mindfulness, and three decades of practical experience from Jane. The beauty of this book is that we are going to keep this simple and straight forward for you.

That's where I come in. My name is Simone Essex; I am a journalist and co-author of *How To Be Yourself*. I am also Jane's daughter and I have benefited from her wisdom, compassion and professional experience my entire life!

My goal is to strip this right back for you and deliver the core content in easy, bite-sized pieces. I understand you want answers quickly along with practical techniques you can use straight away. That's why our book is short and to the point. This means no fluff, just the real answers you want to know.

While *How To Be Yourself* aims to help you overcome your insecurities and strengthen your life, the value of one-on-one therapy with a suitably qualified health care professional should not be underestimated.

If your difficulties with self-confidence are causing you to experience severe depressed moods and anxiety, then we strongly recommend you seek professional help. *How To Be Yourself* and the *Be Yourself Hypnosis* can also be the prefect adjunct to your psychological treatment. We hope you enjoy the journey.

Best wishes,
Jane and Simone

1. The Emotional Cleanse

Have you ever heard someone say 'just be yourself' as though it is the answer to everything? How frustrating! Don't they know how hard it is to be yourself, especially if you don't really know who you are anymore?

In modern busy life, it's easy for you to forget what is important and what really matters. Your values can become lost in the fog of everyday life and it is difficult to navigate your way out again. And is this any wonder, with the endless pressure you put upon yourself to belong to a certain group, look a particular way or achieve remarkable success? You are so busy trying to live up to your own expectations that you neglect the most empowering and meaningful gift of all—to be yourself.

Learn how to clear away unhelpful thoughts and replace them with confident ones whenever you want to.

While happiness is an elusive quality that we all strive for, there is an intrinsic link between being true to yourself and living a happy life. It's our goal to help you develop a strong and healthy relationship with yourself so you can strengthen all aspects of your personal and professional lives. Until you can become confident and comfortable with who you are, unpleasant feelings of discomfort or even anxiety may continue to cloud your view of yourself and the world around you.

As humans we naturally seek approval and acceptance from people around us, it's part of our human nature and you will learn more about that in chapter two. However, we often invest an unhealthy amount of energy into worrying about what others think.

It is unfortunate how widespread this phenomenon is, not only throughout the community, but how far it reaches into each life. It can affect your intimate relationships, friendships, family, career, parenting and other important aspects of your life.

Over-thinking or ruminating on events can lead you to experience unpleasant emotions such as fear, anger, jealousy or inadequacy. You can become so wrapped up in these thoughts and feelings that you begin to believe them with every ounce of your soul. It is a vicious cycle and the birthplace of 'I'll be happy when...'

Have you ever caught yourself out with this one? I'll be happy when... I lose 5 kilograms. I'll feel better about myself when... I get that promotion. I'll be more confident when... I drive that car. With your never ending to-do list is it any wonder being happy with yourself is continually put forward to a future date?

Right now you are too busy and stressed to be yourself, right? Wrong! It's never too late to embrace a new way of thinking and change your life experience for the better. By doing so, you will also enrich the lives of the people that matter to you, as they experience a refreshing and relaxed side of you that perhaps they have not seen for many years.

Remember, happiness is a choice you make. This life is yours. You own it. It belongs to you. So why not take a leap forward, shake off these thoughts and feelings that are holding you back and start to really *live!*

Are you ready for your emotional cleanse? Just like many beauty routines, this is a quick, three step process. It will become second nature to you and you will be able to:

 Step 1. Clear away messy, unhelpful thoughts

 Step 2. Relax and calm your mind

 Step 3. Think more confidently

Imagine how empowering it would be if you could do that!

The three steps are a combination of simple techniques to help you feel relaxed, grounded and confident in more situations. Because everyone is unique, you will have the opportunity to choose from a smorgasbord of proven tools and strategies so you can tailor an emotional cleanse specifically for you. Then you can pop it in the back of your mind and take it with you where ever you go.

We will help you to identify and embrace your personality style, values, strengths and likes, so you can enjoy a clear understanding of who you are in the first place. To make it easy for you, we have designed some simple exercises and worksheets for you to complete so you can discover the answers without even trying.

We will teach you some straightforward and powerful techniques to help you separate yourself from your thoughts and overcome the fear of judgement. All the guesswork has been taken out, right down to scripting suggestions of what you can say to yourself and providing examples of how to use the different techniques.

Plus we're going to share some practical do's and don'ts when it comes to interacting with others, conversation skills, formulating apologies, dealing with difficult people and more. *How To Be Yourself* is a foolproof road map to authentic, lasting change. It truly is possible, once you know how. So take your first step towards a happier life and keep reading this book!

2. The Human Condition

Do you ever lie awake at night worried about what you said yesterday? Does your lack of confidence drag you down at work! Do you fool your family, religion or occupation is stifling your personality but after living this way for so long you have forgotten who you really are?

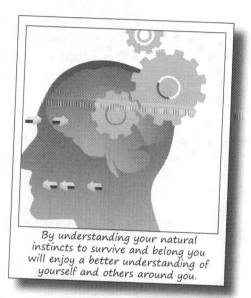

By understanding your natural instincts to survive and belong you will enjoy a better understanding of yourself and others around you.

If so, you are not alone. Thousands upon thousands of people feel exactly the same way. We know this because we ran an online survey and were inundated with responses from people describing the challenges they faced with truly being themselves. The fear of judgement and feeling 'lost' in life were the most common and reoccurring struggles facing our respondents. Psychologist and co-author Jane Briscoe also treats clients with these 'everyday' concerns on a regular basis. It really is common, but how did we end up like this?

First of all, it is important to understand that your yearning to belong, to fit in and be liked is not unique to you—everyone feels the same way. But why? If we all feel the same way why don't we all just relax and be ourselves... say what we want to say and do what we want to do?

The answer lies in the evolution of our species, *Homo sapiens*. When we first appeared on the planet about one hundred thousand years ago, our primitive human mind evolved primarily to protect us from a world filled with danger. Picture yourself as an early human hunter-gatherer, or caveman if you like. Your world is filled with ferocious predators and other life threatening scenarios. Your only concerns are to survive and reproduce.

With this in mind, your primary needs are simply food, water, shelter and sex. Early humans understood that none of this mattered if they were dead, so these needs naturally came second to their main priority—survival!

So in their day-to-day lives, early humans were constantly looking out for danger and actively avoiding it in order to survive. The human mind therefore evolved as a natural survival device.

This survival instinct has proven mighty useful to humans to say the least. As time went on, our ancestors became better and better at identifying and avoiding danger. They started to live longer and were able to have more children.

Like our ancestors, these survival instincts play a role in our lives to this very day. Of course our minds don't warn us about the dangers of vicious man-eating predators these days. Instead, we tend to worry about our relationships, jobs, money, rejection, body image, health and a million other concerns that hound us on a daily basis and commonly for no good reason.

The important thing to understand is that this worry that you may feel from time to time is normal, it is part of the human instinct to survive and protect yourself from danger. However, just because it is normal it doesn't mean you have to struggle with it! Change really is possible and there is no time like the present to let go of the unnecessary worry that is holding you back.

Another ancient human instinct that still affects us today is the need to belong to a group. For the early humans, belonging to a group simply meant life or death. If their clan rejected them and threw them out of their cave, the individual would surely be attacked and killed by a terrifying predator. The human mind therefore evolved a function to avoid rejection from the group... comparison. They started to compare themselves to other people in their clan. Am I good enough? Am I fitting in? Do people like me? Can I contribute something worthwhile? Am I doing anything wrong?

No doubt you can relate to some of that. Our human condition tries to protect us from rejection by instinctively comparing ourselves to those around us. It's like our default setting. Is it any wonder we get distracted and bogged down with these awful thoughts and feelings? Well, it's time to reduce the impact these thoughts have on you because, guess what, the threat of rejection does not result in life or death anymore. It has not been that way for thousands of years, however these instincts are so strong they are repeated generation after generation and interfere with the way we think and interact with other people. The time for change has arrived.

3. Are You Being Yourself?

So what does it mean to 'be yourself' anyway? And when do you know if you *are* being true to yourself or whether deep down you are really only trying to fit in or impress someone? Well first of all, let's take a look at some behaviours that indicate when you are *not* being yourself.

Excessive social comparison can lead to self-defeating behaviour such as altering your appearance or personality style for approval

These may include:

- Changing your opinion to one that is more popular
- Altering your physical appearance and the way you dress to impress people
- Changing your general likes and dislikes such as music, sports and hobbies in order to belong
- Changing your religious or spiritual beliefs for approval
- Rejecting people whom you would normally like
- Spending time with people whom you normally would not like
- Changing your social status and purchasing specific items in order to fit in
- Forcibly shifting your personality style, such as from introvert to extrovert so as to be liked
- Acting very differently in order to appear interesting
- Avoiding doing something you love because of what others may think

If some of these characteristics sound like you, that's okay. Don't feel bad or silly, remember it is *normal* to compare yourself to others and sometimes make adjustments in order to avoid rejection. It is how we have been conditioned as humans for thousands of years.

However, if you continually attempt to control and censor your personality, this self-defeating behaviour will only lead to stress, unhappiness and feelings of discomfort. Perhaps you are feeling this way already? And do you know why? It's because you are taking steps that go against 'who you are'.

Being yourself may mean many different things to each one of you, however a strong indicator is when your actions are aligned with your values. In other words, you do and say what you genuinely believe in, not what you think other people might like. It's fantastic if you know what your values are, but unless you follow through with actions and life decisions that reflect your values, you will inevitably struggle with this inconsistency.

If you have no idea what your values are or how to identify them, don't worry. There is a whole section dedicated to clarifying and using your values in chapter four, so you will be back on track in no time.

Another key element to being yourself is learning how to accept and embrace who you are, right *now*. Acceptance is king! While it may feel good at times to feel in control of your life, your personality or your appearance, it is important to realise that you can't control everything all the time.

Be careful not to misinterpret this message as an endorsement for giving up. That's not what we are saying at all. Of course we encourage you to change whatever you can to create a better life and avoid problems, however it is vital to understand that there are, and will always be, particular aspects of yourself and your life that are out of your control.

If you constantly try to change the unchangeable, you may struggle to enjoy the true freedom of being yourself and being happy. You may also experience unpleasant emotions such as frustration, anger or disappointment at high levels. We are here to help you avoid this.

The essence of this acceptance concept is summarised so well in the Serenity Prayer by theologian Reinhold Niebuhr that we felt it was worth including it right now:

> God grant me the serenity
>
> To accept the things I cannot change;
>
> Courage to change the things I can;
>
> And the wisdom to know the difference.

This prayer or quote is so powerful and effective is has been adopted by various 12 step programs including Alcoholics Anonymous. Why not write it on a post-it note and place it somewhere prominent as a reminder that acceptance, rather than change, is often the wisest option when it comes to being you.

While you are about to feast on a smorgasbord of tools and techniques to help you feel more comfortable with being yourself, the two key concepts we want you to remember for now are your values and acceptance. Let the journey begin!

4. Who Are You?

So, the big question—who are you? What do you love? What are your strengths? What are your dreams? Are you reflective and quiet? Are you bubbly and boisterous? It's important to understand and embrace your own personality, strengths and values so that you can truly relax around others and be yourself.

But before we dive into your personality, it's essential for you to recognize that you are not your past. This point is so important we are going to repeat it—you are not your past. In the past you were a different person in a different time. You are here right now, in the present moment reading this book.

You are made up of many different facets including your personality style, strengths, likes, dislikes and values.

Unfortunately, traumatic and tragic events occur all the time. Perhaps something bad happened to you in the past? These experiences can have a powerful influence over the way you see yourself and how you experience the world around you. If you believe your thoughts, feelings and actions are negatively influenced by a past event, it is a good idea to visit a counsellor, psychologist or your local doctor for some one-on-one assistance. You will be amazed at how light and free you will feel once the baggage of your past has been dropped off at the door.

While this book has not been created to assist you with your past, it is here to partner you in your journey towards overcoming your insecurities and feeling more relaxed, happy and comfortable around others.

First of all we need to roll our sleeves up and get to know your personality style! The great thing about the next exercise is that there is no right or wrong, perfect or preferred personality. Each and every one of us is unique so just relax and be honest with yourself.

The following table gives a very broad generalisation of some common personality characteristics. This is not an extensive list and we will stress again—there is no right or wrong! Read through the list and no doubt you will identify with some characteristics.

Common Personality Characteristics

Extroverted Characteristics	Introverted Characteristics
Like to have people around	Careful with details
Like variety and action	Enjoy being alone
Good communicators	Like quiet time
Tend to process things quickly	Interested in ideas and reasons behind things
Handle interruptions well	Like to think a lot before acting

Sensing Characteristics	Intuitive Characteristics
Like established routine	Dislike repetition
Good attention to detail	Good at problem solving with the 'big picture' in mind
Enjoy using existing skills rather than learning new ones	Reach conclusions quickly
Patient with long or slow tasks	Follow inspirations
Logical step by step thinkers	Patient with complicated situations

Thinking Characteristics	Feeling Characteristics
May be unaware when they hurt someone's feelings	Relate well to most other people
Strong assertiveness skills	Need harmony in relationships
Good analytical thinkers	Enjoy pleasing people, sometimes too much
Need fair treatment	Very aware of how others are feeling
Good concentration skills, not easily distracted	Often sympathetic to others

Judging Characteristics	Perceptive Characteristics
Enjoy structure and predictability	Adapt well to change
Make decisions quickly, sometimes too quickly	Sometimes can be indecisive
Enjoy a sense of satisfaction once a judgement is reached	Delay tasks they dislike
Dislike interruptions, even for something urgent	Curious and open minded to new things and perspectives
Like clear focus until things are finished	Often have many projects on the go at one time

How did you do? Did you find yourself relating to different characteristics across a few different boxes? That's totally normal. In fact the common 16 personality types are all made up of different combinations of these eight groups of personality characteristics.

To find out exactly what personality type you are, we recommend that you complete the internationally recognised Myers-Briggs Type Indicator (MBTI) personality test. It is a free, online, self-scoring test which will tell you what type you are, then you can go and learn all about your personality type. To complete the MBTI test right now, visit: http://www.personalitypathways.com/type_inventory.html

While completing the personality test is beneficial in your journey to get to know yourself better, it is not essential for you to be able to continue with our next exciting exercise about making the most of your strengths.

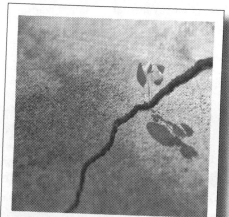

Like the seedling pushing through a crack in the bitumen, success comes when using character strengths such as persistence and perseverance.

Strengths

Acknowledging and using your key strengths is an empowering step towards feeling comfortable and being yourself. Unlike traditional clinical psychology that focuses on solving problems, positive psychology emphasises the importance of identifying and developing your strengths so that you can reach your true potential.

It's amazing how many people do exactly the opposite and focus on 'fixing' their weaknesses to the point they define themselves by all of the things they find difficult. For example, "I'm not a good leader at all, my team doesn't know what it's doing, I'm hopeless." By thinking like this, you are investing all of your energy into a potential weakness (leadership) and no doubt experiencing few positive results in return.

Instead of letting yourself become consumed by worry about whatever it is that frustrates you, try to think more laterally about your strengths. How can you build upon what you are already good at so as to directly, or indirectly assist your perceived weakness? Be creative with your approach rather than driving straight ahead into the same old dead end.

Remember, everyone can't be fabulous at everything. And while you may feel as though you are doing the right thing by wanting to improve your weaknesses, you will actually experience greater results by accepting your ongoing difficulties and focussing on your strengths. Acceptance is the key here, then move on.

A fantastic by-product of doing what you love and focussing on your strengths is that you tend to naturally achieve positive results and excel in these areas. This in turn may lead you to experience feelings of pride, joy, satisfaction and happiness. Also, focussing on your strengths will naturally create a buffer against your weaknesses. This is because the positive results and feelings you experience from excelling in an area of strength tends to overshadow any negative struggle you may have with your weaknesses.

Before we go any further, it is important to understand that strengths are not the same as talents. A strength is a moral trait or a personality characteristic such as kindness, curiosity or creativity. Meanwhile a talent is a non-moral skill such as playing football, ballet dancing or mathematics. Another clear difference between a strength and a talent is you have to choose to use your strength, while a talent may come to you naturally.

Example:

Rachel showed obvious talent in ballet dancing at a young age. Her mother was an elite dancer and it seemed that Rachel had inherited this talent. Although Rachel was destined for a remarkable career in dance, she gave it up during her teenage years because the training and practice became too much work for her. Some may say Rachel wasted her talent in dance because she was lazy. In other words, she chose not to use strengths such as persistence or perseverance.

Meanwhile one of Rachel's dance colleagues, Nicole, was not as talented or gifted a dancer as Rachel. However Nicole had the determination to persevere with the demands of professional dancing and went on to enjoy a magnificent and rewarding career. Nicole focussed her attention on her character strengths (persistence and perseverance) to excel in dance rather than trying to fix a weakness (for example a specific dance technique). In the long term, it is your strengths, not so much your talents that will bring you success and happiness.

If you are interested in finding out how to identify and use your strengths then keep reading! We will show you a quick and easy way to measure your strengths using a simple online test. You will receive your results as soon as you finish so that you can instantly see where your strengths lie and the areas on which you should focus.

Dr. Martin Seligman is the founder of positive psychology and together with the Values-in-Action (VIA) Institute and Christopher Peterson, he has created two online questionnaires that test and measure the 24 signature strengths. The first is the VIA Survey of Character Strengths, very comprehensive with 240 questions to answer. The second is the Brief Strengths Test, which with only 24 questions, is quick and simple to complete. We recommend you start with the Brief Strengths Test for now, and if you wish to, complete the longer version at a later date. Note that both questionnaires test and measure your answers against the same 24 signature strengths so in essence they are very similar.

To take either questionnaire for free, simply visit www.authentichappiness.org and register your name and details. Once you complete the registration form you will be granted instant access to the questionnaires. Go on and give it a go. You may surprise yourself!

Your Top 5 Signature Strengths

Hopefully by now you have completed the Brief Strengths Test. Look at your results and compile a list of your top five best scoring strengths. Keep in mind that no one strength is better or worse than another. Write down your top five here:

Top 5 Signature Strengths
1.
2.
3.
4.
5.

Excellent! Now that you have identified your top five key strengths, it is time to think about how you might use them more often in your day-to-day life. Here's an example from Toby:

Toby's Top 5 Signature Strength Monthly Activities	
Strength 1	Love of learning
Activity 1	I will read a book in an area of interest to me
Strength 2	Vitality
Activity 2	I will visit a place I have never been before
Strength 3	Creativity
Activity 3	I will take a short course in film making
Strength 4	Curiosity
Activity 4	I will read about climate change
Strength 5	Social Intelligence
Activity 5	I will host a dinner party

Whatever your strengths are, think about how you can exercise them in your personal or professional life and write down your ideas. By doing this you will make the most of your strengths and will naturally enjoy yourself and *be* yourself in the meantime.

Your Top 5 Signature Strength Monthly Activities	
Strength 1	
Activity 1	
Strength 2	
Activity 2	
Strength 3	
Activity 3	
Strength 4	
Activity 4	
Strength 5	
Activity 5	

As time goes on, you may find some of these activities will come to you naturally. That's fantastic! Use this opportunity to go back to your Brief Strengths Test results and choose another strength you would like to develop and repeat the exercise above. For best results, review and update your strengths and activities once every month. Remember like anything, the more you practice, the better you will become.

Likes and Dislikes

By giving some focussed thought as to what your likes and dislikes are, we are going to help you get back in touch with some of the important layers that make up who you are. You might have a clear understanding of what it is that you really enjoy, or perhaps you are so busy with day-to-day life that you have forgotten what really makes you tick. Let's find out.

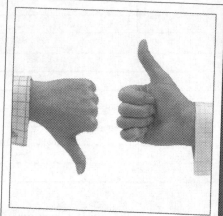

By clarifying your likes and dislikes, it will be easier to stay true to yourself and ideally do more of what you enjoy.

Think about what you are good at or what you would like to be better at. When are you at your happiest? When are you most relaxed? When do you feel most alive? What excites and inspires you? When do you have fun? When are you at peace? What do you like to do in your spare time?

Please focus on activity-based likes rather than people you like. For example, instead of saying 'I like my sister' you might say 'I like clothes shopping with my sister'. Focus on the doing.

We also want you to only consider activities that do not involve the use of alcohol or drugs. These substances have the potential to be extremely detrimental to your physical and mental health. Our aim is to teach you how to have authentic fun and feel enthusiastic about life without the need for an artificial high.

Don't just think about your answers—write them down in the list below. This will help your mind to focus and for you to remember your list of likes.

Here is an example from Toby:

My Likes:
Creating short videos on my computer
Taking my dog to the park on Sunday mornings
Eating out at new restaurants

Okay, now your turn. You can write as many or as few as you like.

My Likes:	

...bout what it is that you dislike doing. You might have to do some of these ...our life but you prefer to do other things. And remember; keep it activity ...instead of people focussed. Get specific and keep it impersonal.

...Toby's example:

Dislikes:
...tting up early in the morning
...oing to the gym
Going to corporate networking events

You know what to do, write it down!

My Dislikes:	

Good. We will come back to this in a moment. First we need to look at your values.

Values

Let's dig a little deeper. It's time to really think about what you want to ach... life. Do you want to be a great parent? Do you want to achieve grand succ... career? Do you want to volunteer for a good cause? What really matters... picture?

Connecting with your values will give your life meaning, purpose an... you to live your life in a valued direction and deliver a sense of ful... life can be challenging at times, however by choosing to live by y... all of your hard work seem worth the effort. In this chapter, w... your values—your heart's deepest desires as to what you war...

First we would like to clarify the difference between a val... or a concept that you choose to live by, on an ongoing b... it may evolve, but it is an overall 'principle' that you c... activity that you work towards then cross off your lis...

For example, you might value healthy living. To b... three times per week. Exercising three times a v... your list and it contributes to your overall valu... here is focus on your values, not your goals. ... in itself so we want to stay focussed on your v...

What rea...

This is an ...

no right or ...

we want you...

Here is an ex...

My Values:
1. My relationship...
2. Learning new t...
3. Being outdoors,...

How To Be Yourself

Another point to consider is that feelings are not values. Feel[ings] they are good or bad. So to 'feel happy' is actually a goal t' achieve by connecting with your *values*. For example, yo[u] lifestyle that goes with it. The surfing lifestyle is therefore w. by-product of surfing more often, is that you feel happy. If you . thinking or writing about how you would like to feel, ask yourself, way, what would you be doing differently? The answers to this questi. uncover your values.

Let's get started. If you need to, move yourself to a quiet location where you . interrupted and give this some honest consideration. Think about:

- What is important to you?
- What are you passionate about?
- What sort of person would you like to be?
- What do you want your life to focus on?

It is okay if you don't have all the answers straight away, don't get flustered—just take your time. You might like to think about particular areas of your life such as:

- Family relationships
- Intimate relationships
- Parenting
- Friendships
- Career
- Education and learning
- Recreation and fun
- Spirituality
- Creativity
- Environment and community
- Health and well-being

[rea]lly matters to you?

[e]xercise that you can come back to and fine tune over time. Remember there is [no] wrong answers and you can always make changes as you grow, but right now, [try] to list just three things in life that you value.

[exa]mple from Toby:

[..] with my parents	
[..]hings	
[..] appreciating nature	

You see it doesn't have to be complicated, just list at least three aspects of your life that are important to you. The simple act of writing them down will truly help you identify with these values a whole lot more than if you just think about them. Come on, you have nothing to lose.

My Values:
1.
2.
3.

Excellent, now we are getting somewhere! The following exercise is where this all comes together. You are going to write an email to a long lost cousin. You will never send the email and your 'long lost cousin' obviously doesn't exist, this is simply an exercise to help you to get to know yourself.

Email to Jeremy

Your long lost cousin, Jeremy, managed to track you down online. You haven't seen Jeremy since you were about nine years old. You and Jeremy were the best of buddies and used to talk about what you wanted to be when you grew up.

You were surprised and excited to receive the email from Jeremy. He is very interested to re-connect with you and wants to know all about you and your life. He's asking the very questions that your strengths, likes, dislikes and values list can answer. Perfect! The hard work is done, all you have to do combine these lists into a self-descriptive email and Jeremy will be fully up to date! Feel free to add details about yourself that are not in your lists above. The purpose of this exercise is for you to be honest and open in describing yourself to someone who WILL NOT JUDGE YOU. Right now it is your long lost cousin Jeremy.

Here is an example from Toby:

Wow, so good to hear from you! Yes my parents are really well thanks. I hope yours are too? I moved out of home a few years ago and we get along better than ever. We usually meet at the park on a Sunday morning. I take my dog Rambo and throw a ball for him—I've attached a photo of Rambo, what a legend!

No, I don't have a girlfriend but to be honest I'm okay with that. Someone will come along. My mum is always at me to exercise, look after myself and get out there, blah, blah. She even bought me a gym membership! I went to the gym a few times but I really don't like it and I hate getting up early. Do you work out? Remember you used to want to be a fireman? Did you do it?

I just got a new job in an advertising agency. So far it's pretty good but they make me go to these corporate networking events where I'm meant to go and meet new people and turn them into clients. I really hate doing that stuff, I feel so fake! I guess you have to take the good with the bad! Hey, I've been creating some short videos and posting them on YouTube, you should check them out, pretty funny! Although they're a bit basic, I've just enrolled in a short film course to help me with creating better special effects. Should be great! I've also been reading some books in this area, hopefully one day I will get to make a feature length film...

Hey, thanks for the invitation to come and stay with you, I've never been to your town and I love visiting places I have never been before! What's the weather been like down there? It's been crazy up here, from floods to droughts to fires. This climate change stuff is really taking its toll, I want to find out more about it, there's got to be more we can do to stop it!

Anyway, what's going on with you? If you're up this way let me know, I'll get some of my friends together and I'll throw a dinner party. I'm quite the chef you know! Looking forward to hearing from you.

Toby

Now it's your turn to write to Jeremy about your life. He is genuinely interested in you and how you have grown up. He wants to know what you like, what you don't like, what you value and what direction you are heading in. He will not judge you or mock you—it is time to be honest. What easier topic is there than to write about yourself? It doesn't need to be a long, elaborate message, just a current and honest snapshot of you.

Go on, it is your turn:

Hi Jeremy,

See that wasn't so hard!

Now you are more familiar with your strengths, likes, dislikes and values, it will be so much easier to stay true to yourself because you have a better understanding of who you are in the first place. Well done! It is also important to understand that while you might have a better idea of who you are, it's normal that you will not feel the same all the time. Let's explore this further.

Self is State Dependent

What we mean by your 'self is state dependent' is that your 'self' changes depending on your environment and who you are with. It is normal to feel different when you are in a variety of situations and interacting with different people.

Let's take Sally for example:

Sally is a young I.T. Manager at a medium-sized company. She is good at her job and feels comfortable with her workload and ability to solve the I.T. problems that arise on a day-to-day basis. In fact she does such a good job, that her employer nominated her for a young businesswomen's achievement award.

Sally won the award, had her photo in the paper and was asked to speak to a group of I.T. managers in her local business network group about her innovative systems. Many of the I.T. specialists she was to present to were a lot older than her with more experience. Sally began to feel more and more uncertain about her ability and her 'worthiness' as a speaker. She began to dread giving the presentation and even the thought of it put butterflies in her stomach...

Isn't it funny how she is doing this to herself? She is so good at her job that she won an award and received media coverage for her achievement, yet she doesn't feel good enough to speak in front of people who are on her level. This is why we say that your 'self' is state dependent—the way you feel and act depends on where you are and whom you are with. Remember Sally felt comfortable and happy in her workplace doing what she does best, but take her out of this comfort zone and she begins to doubt herself. This is normal and this book will teach you some strategies to help you develop lifelong skills to feel more at ease in more situations.

Before we go any further, let's take a moment to summarise who 'you' are. You are a combination of:

- **Your personality characteristics**
- **Your strengths**
- **Your likes**
- **Your dislikes**
- **Your values**

We also learnt that 'you' are state dependent and will therefore think, feel and act differently depending on your situation. We hope that the exercises in this chapter helped you to get in touch with who you are and perhaps even learn something about yourself. With a better understanding of yourself, you are now in a stronger psychological position to overcome the fear of judgement that you may experience from time to time.

5. Fear of Judgement

A key step to overcoming the fear of judgement is to get out of your mind and take more notice of what happens around you.

I wonder what they're thinking. I bet they've all been talking about me...I shouldn't have said that yesterday... maybe I should have said this...

You have been there, right? Concerned about what other people think and say about you to the point it replays over and over in your mind? The unfortunate thing is that as humans, we often hold this false belief that everyone must like us all the time. However just as people have different preferences in the food they eat, the places they visit and the occupations they follow, they too have different preferences in the types of people they like. It's normal and natural to gravitate towards a certain style of person. No doubt you do this without even realising it and everyone else does it too. This does not mean that the other people are bad, imperfect or unlovable; it simply means that you might not be the right fit together.

It really is just like shopping for fruit at the market. It is most likely you don't buy every type of fruit available; you only buy the fruit that you like to eat. Take Toby for example, he only likes apples, and not just any apples, he only likes green apples. It doesn't mean that the red apples he leaves behind are bad or rotten, he simply prefers green apples. To the next person who comes along, those red apples will look delicious! Now the same goes for you, if you believe someone may not be too fond of you, that is okay! It doesn't mean you are bad or unlovable; you simply may not be the type of person they naturally gravitate towards. Remember the belief that everyone must like you all the time is false and unrealistic.

Like any fear, the fear of judgement can rise and fall to different degrees depending on the individual and the situation. For some, it can grip with such force that they completely avoid certain situations like parties, dates or public speaking because they get overwhelmed with worry about what people might think of them. What a waste! Think of all the amazing things in life you will miss out on if you react in this way.

The truth is it's quite common for people to feel nervous about meeting new people or speaking to a group. It is okay if you feel like that from time to time but we are here to help you push through those feelings so you can start to feel more at ease in more situations.

Firstly, it's important to understand that the fear of judgement is more internally focussed rather than externally influenced. Meaning, the fear and insecurities you experience exist in your mind and not in the world around you. They are caused by over monitoring activities and over analysing thoughts and emotions. This in turn can lead to over monitoring fear symptoms and then you are back to the start, like a vicious cycle. It is important not to always believe what you think about yourself. The mind is like a word machine and we have many stories about ourselves that spin around and often they are not true, accurate or logical.

Acceptance and Commitment Therapy (ACT) is a relatively new therapy model founded by pioneering psychologist Steven Hayes. ACT aims to provide you with psychological flexibility so you can disengage from your thoughts and connect with your life at the present moment. As humans, we often become glued or fused to our thoughts and we mistakenly interpret these thoughts as confirmation of who we are. As a result, these thoughts often prevent us from taking steps towards living a happier, more meaningful life.

Don't become alarmed when distracting, unhelpful thoughts arise. Instead of struggling with these thoughts, accept them as part of being human. Be aware of them, notice how they make you feel, but do not allow them to immobilize you. Move forward in a valued direction so that you can bring purpose and meaning to your life. Remember identifying your values in chapter four? This is what it is all about! By enjoying a clear understanding of your values it is easier to take purposeful action in your life that reflects what you believe in rather than succumbing to the doom and gloom voice of your insecurities.

So if your value direction is to make more friends, expect that the old glum thoughts like "he must think I'm foolish" will pop up from time to time. The difference is from now on, you will be able to clearly identify the thought for what it is—just a silly thought from your 'word machine' mind—and unhook yourself from it by saying to yourself:

"There's that thought about ..."

You will be amazed how powerful this strategy alone can be. By being *aware* of the thought and *identifying* it as "that thought about..." you are effectively separating yourself from your thoughts. What an empowering result from something so simple! We urge you to give it a go. Remember, thoughts and feelings are things we experience, they are not who we are.

Mindfulness techniques can also help you to disconnect from your thoughts and focus more on the present moment. In chapter seven we will teach you some powerful mindfulness techniques to help you focus more on your external world so you can feel more calm and grounded. But in the meantime, let's see how Toby reacts to his fear of judgement when a group of new people he would like to impress invite him out for a drink.

Toby has just started a new job in a trendy office in the city. It's been a big week of learning new things and meeting new people. He has been somewhat nervous because everyone dresses so cool and he feels a bit out of touch. It is Friday afternoon, the team are going out for a drink and they invited Toby along. The thought of socialising with these people literally frightened him. What would he say? They're all such close friends. Would they like him? He's not dressed right! But despite these thoughts he accepted the offer.

You can never be certain about what others think of you, so relax and focus on the present moment.

Toby wanted to make a good impression, especially on Mike who always seemed so easy going and fun. He wanted to become part of the group and join in the conversation but was so worried about what they were thinking of him that he barely said a word the entire time. The longer he didn't say anything, the more nervous and quiet he became.

Meanwhile on the other side of the table, Toby's new colleague Jess has taken a fancy to Toby and wants to get to know him better. She's curious about what he's thinking and misinterprets his silence as boredom. This makes Jess nervous so she launches into story and after story and finds herself talking a lot to fill the silences. She really wants Toby to like her so she wants to appear fun and interesting.

And then there's Mike. He's sitting there with them, enjoying a nice cold drink after a hard day's work. He's half listening to Jess's stories while keeping one eye on the football score and another on his mobile phone. He's expecting a call soon but he's not concerned there's plenty of time for another drink...

Perhaps you are familiar with this type of scenario? Not surprisingly it is very common for people to convince themselves that *everyone* is watching them and forming opinions about them. Meanwhile someone on the other side of the room is worried about what you are thinking of *them*. And then there are the people who are not deep in thought and are simply distracted by the present activities and having a good time.

The reality is, you can never be certain about what people are thinking, or if they are thinking about you at all. And the key thing to respect here is that you can never control what others think. Remember the Serenity Prayer from chapter two? Forcing yourself to change in an attempt to influence others to think better of you really is a waste of time and energy. At the end of the day, people will think whatever they want to think. The most important thing is for you to respect others and respect yourself.

So come on! Don't over analyse what people *might* be thinking because you will never really know unless you ask them, and even then you can't be sure you will get an accurate answer.

It is best to disconnect from your thoughts, relax and focus your attention on the present activities.

Here is a helpful summary of the key points to remember when you feel the fear of judgement rise up inside of you:

- Everyone won't like you all the time

- Get out of your mind and focus on the external world around you

- Don't always believe what you think about yourself

- Say to yourself 'there's that thought about...' when distressing thoughts arise

- Not everyone is forming opinions about you all the time

- You can never be certain about what others think

- You can never control what others think

- Focus your attention on the present activities

- Fully engage with what you are presently doing

6. A Healthy Amount of Concern

While many of us worry too much about what others think, please understand only sociopaths and psychopaths do not care at all what people think. That's why they often follow through with horrific actions, because they have absolutely no regard for others.

So we are not here to teach you how to 'not care' what others think. Instead we want to show you how to have a healthy amount of concern for others.

But where do you start and stop? How do you know when you are placing too much importance on what someone is thinking? Well, it can be tricky, but we are about to teach you a strategy that Jane Briscoe has used with her clients for many years and with lots of success.

Stop worring about what EVERYONE thinks of you and only pay attention to the people that MATTER by using the Stick of Judgement.

It is called the Stick of Judgement.

The Stick of Judgement is a stick that will live in your mind. Take a moment to visualise your Stick. It is a strong, thick Stick, like a baton athletes use when they run a relay race. The Stick is very sacred to you because whoever holds the Stick has your permission to give you feedback.

The only way someone can hold your Stick is if you pass it over, and you have the power to get it back at any time. You are in complete control. The key here is to only pass your stick to a special group of people, not just anyone. In a moment you will write a list of these people and reasons why they are included on your list.

Now think very carefully about the people in your life. Whoever you include on the list will hold your Stick of Judgement from time to time and you will listen with respect to their feedback and comments about you and your life.

You will listen to them and consider their thoughts because you are choosing to, because you have given them your Stick of Judgement and you value their opinion. This does not mean you always have to agree or do as they say, but the key objective is to listen and consider their opinion with a healthy amount of concern.

So who goes on the list?

Include three to five people who are in your life and meet any or all of the following criteria:

- You value their opinion
- You admire their strengths
- You aspire to be like them

Please be sure to include real people in your life and refrain from listing celebrities or other public figures who you do not know personally. The people you choose should generally be people you are close to and interact with on a regular basis.

Give this some careful consideration, but please don't stall. Take action right now, pick up a pen and write down your three to five people and, for each one, the one main reason you have included them on your list. Here is an example from Sally.

Person	Reason
Mum	I value her opinion about my big life decisions and life direction
Dad	I admire his strength when he's faced with hard times
Brother	I value his opinion of my choice of boyfriends
Best Friend	I aspire to be more like Sonia because she is so relaxed and happy
Employer	I value his opinion of my work ability

Okay, now it is your turn. Pick up your pen and write your list. You can do it in your mind, but it really will be more effective if you complete the exercise and write it down. Go on!

Person	Reason

How it Works

What tends to happen in day-to-day life is we give our Stick of Judgement to people we don't really respect. We let it go into the hands of the wrong people and become concerned about what the wrong people think. Take Sally for example. Remember how she won the award for her work but felt terrified about speaking to people she perceived as more knowledgeable than her?

With the Stick of Judgement, Sally would be empowered to challenge her fear and revisit her judgement list. Was a room of anonymous I.T. specialists on her list? No, of course not! But you know who was; her employer! It is only his opinion of her work ability that matters to her and remember she only won the award because he nominated her. You see! With the Stick of Judgement Sally realised that the thoughts and opinions of the I.T. specialists did not really matter, because the only opinions that really matter to her are from the people on her list.

Sally gave her speech and she even performed some live demonstrations of her new software system. At first Sally still felt a bit nervous, this is normal, but what she did not experience was the gut wrenching fear and anxiety about what they would all think and say about her afterwards. It didn't matter any more because all that mattered to Sally was that her employer thought she was doing an excellent job. This is the power of the Stick of Judgement.

When you practice using the Stick in your everyday life, you will notice that you keep accidentally giving it to people who are not on your list. This is normal and you should expect it to happen from time to time. The main thing is to be aware of when it happens and be sure to take the stick back from them so you can stop worrying about their opinion.

Handing Your Stick Over

Sometimes life presents a complex fork in the road or a challenge that seems simply too large to tackle on your own. You need to make a decision and you have no idea what to do or where to start. This is where the Stick of Judgement really begins to help shape your life because now you have a starting point—your list! Choose someone from your list who you believe would have some experience or valuable insight into your situation. Contact that person and talk openly with them, explain what is challenging you and ask them what they think. By simply having this conversation, you are effectively handing over your Stick of Judgement to that person. Be sure to listen to their response with respect.

Remember, when we say with respect, it does not mean you have to literally do what that person says, you do not even have to agree, but it is important that you properly listen to their comments with a healthly amount of concern. After all, you did include them on your list for a good reason.

To help you stay focussed and calm during situations such as these, we are going to teach you the practice of mindfulness. You will learn specific techniques to help you unhook from negative thoughts so you can interact positively with the people around you and be yourself.

7. Mindfulness and Re-regulating Your Emotional System

What is Mindfulness?

Mindfulness is a therapeutic application of ancient Buddhist meditation principles. Developed by modern psychology and psychiatry, mindfulness is the practice of actively directing your attention to the here-and-now present moment in a careful and deliberate manner. By doing so, you create an enhanced state of awareness which is what we call mindfulness. Being mindful enables you to direct your attention towards a positive and purposeful outcome.

Mind*less*ness is the direct opposite. A busy life running on autopilot may have many mindless moments peppered throughout each day. Have you ever

Create a calm and spacious mind whenever you want to by practicing a simple mindfulness exercise.

driven home from work and could not recall the journey? Have you ever eaten your lunch and not remembered what it tasted like?

These are common examples of what may happen when your thoughts distract your attention to such a degree that it stops you from fully engaging in your present activities. You might be familiar with the sayings "I was lost in thought" or "I was a million miles away". You might say something like this if perhaps a question was directed at you and you didn't realise you were being spoken to. You may have been so distracted by your own thoughts that you weren't really present.

In this chapter we are going to teach you some key mindfulness techniques to help you tame those unhelpful thoughts and re-regulate your emotional system. It sounds more complex than it is. We are simply going to show you how to draw attention to your senses—sight, sound, smell, touch and taste—so you can better connect with the present moment and therefore moderate your thoughts.

Experts in the field of mindfulness agree that how we focus our attention directly helps to shape the mind. The purpose of teaching you about mindfulness is not so you can strictly control your mind, but so you learn how to shape it and gently massage it into something more calm and pleasant. As humans, we need to exercise our minds and keep them fit, just like our bodies. Mindfulness exercises are perfect to build your mental fitness. It not only helps to keep your mind spacious, calm and focussed, but it also enables your mind to perform at its best during difficult times.

Imagine an unfit, overweight, heavy smoker running to catch the bus. It is likely they will struggle, possibly miss the bus and ruin their morning schedule. Meanwhile a fit and healthy person may find it easy to jog the last 200 metres to catch the bus and carry on with their day. If you maintain a healthy level of physical fitness, you will be able to enjoy the benefits when you least expect to, like when running to catch the bus. The same goes for your mental fitness. It's important to practice mindfulness exercises even when you are feeling well so you can benefit from your mental fitness when you need it most.

Re-regulating Your Emotional System

When you fall into the bad habit of entertaining unhelpful or negative thoughts, your emotions may escalate to feelings of confusion, tension or anxiety. This can in turn lead to poor concentration levels and increases the difficulty of negotiating your way through the maze of who you are.

Does he like me?
I wonder what she thinks about me?
Will I get invited?

It is thoughts like these that can bog you down and cause unnecessary distress. It's important to be able to focus your attention on something more useful so you can calm down and become emotionally stable. A great way to do this is to practice a mindfulness exercise.

Practicing Mindfulness

To be mindful or to practice mindfulness, you don't need to sit crossed legged in a quiet location like the stereotypical meditation position. You can practice mindfulness on your morning walk, in the shower or even sitting at your desk. It really is the perfect meditation for busy people because you can practice on the run and experience instant results.

Imagine for a moment you are at work, you have a lot to do today but your attention keeps wandering back to what happened last night. You keep replaying what was said and you think about what you wish you said. The thoughts keep replaying over and over until an uncomfortable feeling settles over you. You can't concentrate on your job and you have even made a few mindless errors...

The first step to becoming stable in a situation like this is to become aware of your thoughts and feelings. If you are not aware of them, how can you possibly take action to improve them? Notice what you are thinking and how it makes you feel.

Next, focus on your breathing. Take five long, slow, belly breaths in through the nose and out through the nose. Notice what your breath feels like as you breathe in, pay attention to the sound it makes when you breathe out. As your mind no doubt starts to wander back to your negative thoughts, simply notice what your mind is doing and gently bring your attention back to your breathing, in through the nose and out through the nose. Notice the temperature of the air as you breathe in as compared to the temperature of the air as you breathe out. Notice the rise and fall of your stomach as you breathe. Continue to bring your focus back to your breathing every time your mind starts to wander. This is like pressing the slow motion button on your thoughts.

Now give your full attention to the task at hand, whatever it is that you may be doing. If you are typing a letter, imagine it is for the president or prime minister of your country, imagine it is the most important letter you have ever typed and every single keyboard stroke needs to be accurate. Or perhaps you are cooking dinner for your family, imagine Her Majesty the Queen of England is joining you and it is the most important meal you have ever cooked. Notice how the knife slices through the vegetables and focus on cutting thick, even pieces. Immerse yourself in your activities as though the outcome is much more important than it is. This will help to give you to focus on the present moment and distract your mind from unhelpful thoughts.

Another quick and easy way to practice mindfulness is to focus on your senses. Try some of these exercises:

1. **As you walk through the streets, notice five different smells and name them**

2. **As you look out the window, notice five different shades of green**

3. **As you go on your morning walk, notice five different sounds and name them**

4. **As you eat your meals notice the textures and name the different flavours**

5. **As you wash your hair, notice the sensation of your fingers on your scalp and the warm water on your back.**

You can create your own exercises using any of the senses that work in with whatever it is that you are doing at the time. Focus on the detail of the present moment in a non-judgemental way. Simply notice things without judgement, without opinion. You will find your mind floating back to whatever thoughts were bothering you; this is normal but the more you practice, the less this will happen. You can gently bring your mind back to your senses and connect fully with what you are doing. By doing this, you will feel more calm and focussed with a clear mind. This creates a better opportunity for more helpful thoughts to arise so you can relax and be yourself.

8. How to Interact With Others

Do you ever feel awkward around others because you are not really sure how to act or what to say? This is a very common experience; especially when you are in a social setting with lots of new people or people you hardly know. We are going to teach you some basic do's and don'ts that are extremely helpful in social situations. While they may seem obvious for some, they really do work. The key objective is for you to focus less on yourself and more on others around you. Okay—so less thinking and analysing and more awareness and actions.

To relax and feel more comfortable, pay less attention to yourself and more attention to those around you.

How to focus *less* on you and focus *more* on others

Do's	Don'ts
Enjoy yourself	Try to impress
Smile	Try to get people to like you
Connect with someone	Try to be the best
Pursue interesting conversation	Focus on your physical image
Recognise good networking opportunities	Grovel and be a 'people pleaser'
Ask questions	Make others uncomfortable on purpose
Become task orientated, be helpful	
Have an external focus, notice what is happening	

Let's take a closer look:

DO'S

Enjoy yourself

If you are going out, think positively about the event before you arrive—if you tell yourself it will be awful and you are going to feel uncomfortable, guess what, that is exactly what will happen! Instead tell yourself it is going to be a fun time where you can practice using your Stick of Judgement if nothing else!

Smile

People who do not smile are often misinterpreted by others to be arrogant, stuck up or angry. This is obviously not always the case. Many people don't smile because they are shy or nervous. So practice smiling when you greet people and when you talk, plus everyone looks more approachable when they smile.

Connect with someone

Give yourself a healthy challenge and engage yourself in a conversation with someone. Make a point to ask questions and see if you can find some common ground, something you both can relate to.

Pursue interesting conversation

You don't need to discuss politics or religion but you can experience wonderful surprises if you push yourself just a touch and ask thoughtful questions. Refer to chapter nine on conversation skills for some ideas.

Recognise good networking opportunities

It's always great to expand your network of friends and acquaintances. Think laterally and you might find a new business contact at a birthday party or make a new friend at a boardroom meeting. You will never know if you stick with people you already know. Get out of your comfort zone and grow!

Ask questions

The most effective way to start a conversation is to simply ask questions. Most importantly, ask open-ended questions that can't be answered with a yes or no response. This also helps to put your focus on other people and distracts your mind from thinking too much about yourself.

Become task orientated

Place your focus on the task at hand and the activities around you. Be helpful—see if you can lend a hand to someone who is busy.

Have an external focus

Pay attention to the activities around you and notice what is happening. Absorb yourself in your surroundings and be aware of the sights, sounds and smells.

DON'TS

Try to impress

By actively trying to impress people, you are in essence changing yourself or putting on an act so as to gain approval from others. This behaviour is insincere and transparent—people will see through it.

Try to get people to like you

Pay attention to non-verbal cues, don't interrupt other conversations and be considerate of people's personal space. Forcing yourself on others will only push them further away.

Try to be the best

Life isn't a competition! There is no need to attempt to be the best at everything all the time. Competitive behaviour can be very off putting and often makes others feel uncomfortable. Relax! It's also not nice to brag about yourself. Be aware of your audience, the people around you may not have the opportunity to do the great things that you can.

Focus on physical image

If you spend large amounts of time and energy worrying about how you look, you are not only focussing on your internal world, you are effectively blocking out opportunities for fun activities or interesting conversation. After all it is your actions and words that people remember, not your outfit.

Grovel

Don't become a 'people pleaser' and do anything for others specifically so that they like you. This behaviour speaks volumes and says you do not respect yourself. Over time your personality will become so diluted that others will lose track of who you really are and no doubt you will feel the same way about yourself.

Make others uncomfortable

Don't purposefully make other people feel uncomfortable. This is never subtle and people will see through this behaviour for what it is. It displays an unattractive side of you and if you accidentally make someone uncomfortable, it is best to apologise. See chapter eleven for tips on how to apologise to someone.

What people don't like about others

Based on the experience and insight Jane Briscoe has gained in 30 years of practicing psychology in Australia, we have created a quick list of the general behaviours that others tend to dislike. These include people who:

- Talk too much—appear self obsessed
- Don't ask questions—appear self obsessed
- Talk about others a lot—gossip
- Only talk about a single topic—appear boring
- Are too quiet—give only yes or no answers
- Are too loud—appear overbearing
- Are too tense—not smiling
- Are easily distracted—interrupt and look around
- Disregard personal space—sit or stand too close
- Exaggerate stories or tell lies—fake

If you are feeling a bit overwhelmed with all of these do's and don'ts and dislikes that's okay! Just stick with us, as we are about to teach you some rock solid conversation skills so you will become calmer and more at ease talking with new people.

9. Conversation Skills

Core conversation skills include showing interest, asking questions, listening to the answers, making eye contact and smiling.

The value of small talk is often underestimated. People sometimes think of themselves as above small talk, however it is actually a key social skill that leads to deeper, more meaningful conversation.

It is very difficult to approach someone you don't know well and start asking in-depth or specific questions about their life. First you must develop a friendly rapport, and small talk is perfect for this.

'How do you know Toby?'

'I love your shoes. Where did you get them?'

'Your dog looks so fit and healthy; how do you train him?'

'You're great on the guitar. How did you learn to play?'

It is like a game of tennis—you take turns at speaking and asking questions. When someone asks you a question, do more than simply provide an answer. Volunteer extra information and expand your answers as far as you are comfortable. Good communication requires skills and input from both sides to keep up the flow. If you have just asked a question, it is very important that you listen to the other person. This might seem basic, but be sure to properly focus on the answer, make eye contact and show genuine interest. It is usually within the answer to your question that you will find another thread to pick up and weave into another question or comment, and therefore allow the conversation to progress.

It's also a great idea to use someone's name, especially when you meet and greet someone or when saying goodbye. This is polite and shows manners, but be careful not to over do it. If you have forgotten someone's name, don't be shy to ask them to remind you. Most people understand and have been in the same situation themselves.

Stay focussed and friendly. It is amazing how contagious a smile can be. Don't fidget with your clothes, check your phone or look around. Pay attention to the person in front of you; this is basic manners and shows respect.

Think for a moment about your friends and family. Why do you think you are closer with some people than with others? Why do you enjoy spending time with them? Often it's because they show an interest in you. They ask you questions, listen to you and make sure you are healthy and happy. This is a key point to remember when you would like to make a new friend: show interest. Ask questions, listen to the answers, make eye contact and smile.

Another powerful conversation skill is to remember something about a person so that the next time you see them, you can ask a relevant question. This demonstrates that you really were listening last time and that you are interested in them.

Example:
Toby Remembers Something!

Since the night out for drinks with his colleagues, Toby has started to feel more comfortable at his new workplace and is enjoying the attention from Jess. He would like to get to know her better. One day he saw her in the lunchroom and asked her a question.

'What do you have planned for the weekend?'

Simple, right?

She said she was going water skiing with her family this Saturday. Toby told Jess he had never tried water skiing and asked her where they go skiing, which led to a great five-minute chat. When Toby saw Jess at work on Monday, he remembered her plans to go water skiing on the weekend. Toby approached Jess and asked how she had enjoyed her weekend skiing with her family. This was a great way to start a conversation and demonstrated that he was interested.

Don't be disheartened if you do all the right things and receive little in return. Stick with it! Many people have never learnt these core conversation skills and they do not intend to be rude to you even though it may come across that way. The main thing is you were socially intelligent enough to give it a go. Remember, quality conversation is a two-way street.

Self-Disclosure

The next level of friendship and conversation often involves some kind of self-disclosure. Self-disclosure is when you share something about yourself with another person; usually it is something you consider personal. Have you ever noticed how much closer to a person you feel when he or she opens up to you? It makes you feel as though that person trusts and respects you.

Some people take a long time to feel comfortable enough with a new friend to disclose anything about themselves. This can lead to close friendships taking a very long time to formulate. On the other hand, others may disclose personal details too soon out of nervousness and then regret it later. Be careful not to disclose too much information too early in a friendship; just ease your way into the big topics over time. At the same time, try not to guard yourself too closely, otherwise you might run the risk of blocking people out of your life and alienating yourself. You'll know what is right for you; there is no set right or wrong.

By now we hope you have picked up some practical ideas and strategies to help you feel more comfortable around others. But what if you are faced with a difficult situation, confrontation or conflict where no amount of being yourself will help? Well you are probably like the majority of people and don't really enjoy confrontation. For some extra guidance and practical tips on how to develop assertiveness, check out the next chapter.

10. How to Develop Assertiveness

It is common for people to feel flustered and intimidated by strong, domineering people. Confrontation can be overwhelming and scary at times, however if you do not stand up for yourself you will become increasingly unhappy and other areas of your life will suffer, such as your job or your personal relationships.

The main culprit for this is rumination. If you continually neglect to stand up for yourself, you might dwell on events and replay confrontations and conflicts over and over with a strong 'I should have' theme. We have all done it, right? You experience some kind of confrontation

There is a distinct difference between assertion and aggression and while they both may involve sticking up for your rights, the similarities end there.

and you can't think of what to say because you are so flustered or shocked. Then later, you begin to think of all the things you should have said and feel foolish or frustrated.

Next, anger tends to build which could result in an explosion of emotion either directed towards the other person or towards yourself. Both results are undesirable and completely avoidable if a few of our assertiveness skills are practiced.

A key point to remember is that assertiveness does not mean fighting and yelling. In fact you will achieve better results if you do not raise your voice at all but instead keep a calm, non-aggressive approach. There is a distinct difference between assertion and aggression. While they both may involve sticking up for your rights, the similarities end there.

Aggressive people want to win at all costs, regardless of how it affects others. Aggression may include using threats, personal abuse or manipulation. Assertive people want to win, but not at unreasonable costs to others. Assertion may include giving feedback about how the other person's behaviour affects you or highlighting real world consequences rather than using personal abuse or threats.

So the key difference between aggression and assertion is how much you consider other people before you speak and act. It's about finding the balance between being submissive (putting others first too much) and being aggressive (having little regard for others).

The other main difference between aggression and assertion is how it looks and sounds. Your body language and the way you use your voice can have a huge affect on the way someone interprets your words. Aggression is typically harsh and noisy while assertion is often quiet but still firm.

So how do you keep calm when you are gripped by strong emotions such as fear or anger? The first step is to notice the emotion rise up inside of you. Notice if your heart rate increases, notice if the blood rushes to your face. Become fully aware of how you are feeling and refrain from reacting to it or blurting out the first thing that comes to your mind. Instead focus on your breathing, take five big belly breaths and fill your lungs with fresh air as if you were about to blow up a balloon. You are probably emotionally flooded at this point, so the breathing will help to re-regulate your emotional system. This in turn will help you to calm down so that you can properly plan what you will say.

In summary, it is best to:

- **Notice your emotions**
- **Stay calm and non-aggressive**
- **Refrain from acting spontaneously**
- **Focus on your breathing**
- **Clear your mind**
- **Plan what you will say**

Keep in mind you don't always need to respond there and then. You might achieve greater results if you raise the topic at later date, or it might be a recurring situation where you can respond next time once you have properly planned what you will say.

What Do You Say?

When you are choosing your words, it is important to start with a clear mind. You can achieve this by following the steps above or choosing your favourite mindfulness exercise from chapter seven. This will help distract your mind from your emotions and direct your attention to the task at hand—planning what to say.

It is important to ensure your comments are not at the expense of someone else's feelings, even if you were hurt first. Don't hurt someone else just to stand up for yourself. By doing this you are creating a vicious cycle and it is not healthy. Remember the difference between aggression and assertion? It doesn't matter who said what first.

Instead focus on exactly what you want to achieve. Would you like an apology? Do you want someone to know how you feel? Do you need a specific action from someone? By identifying your desired end result, you can then work backwards and plan what to say to achieve this result.

Another strategy is to keep your language 'I' focussed, such as 'I feel ignored when you don't spend time with me at the weekend.' By doing this you are being responsible for your own feelings and not blaming someone else.

For example, if you said 'You always play golf every single weekend and you never give two thoughts as to what I might like to do at the weekend, it's just so selfish!' you start off in 'attack' mode which will instantly put the other person in 'defence' mode and conflict is likely to arise. So be sure to have ownership over your own feelings and do not blame someone else for 'making you' feel a certain way.

Always keep in mind that you have choices in how you think, feel and act. Realise that other people do not cause you to think, feel or act in certain ways even though it may feel that way in the heat of the moment. The way you respond and react to people around you is in your complete control. You must own your thoughts, feelings and actions and take full responsibility for them.

Consider that you do not need to do all of the talking. Try to ask questions and find out what the other person thinks about the topic. By giving the other person a chance to talk, you may also gain insight into why they acted the way in which they did, which could in turn affect your own response to the situation. This will help to keep the conversation fair and balanced.

Now take a moment to visualise your encounter, mentally rehearse what you will say and how you will say it. Give thought to how the other person might react, and visualise being calm and in control, even if the other person is not happy.

When the time comes for you to stand up for yourself or to handle a situation assertively, remember our key points:

- **Notice your emotions**
- **Stay calm and non-aggressive**
- **Refrain from acting spontaneously**
- **Clear your mind**
- **Plan what you will say**
- **Identify your desired outcome**
- **Keep your language 'I' focussed**
- **Ask questions**
- **Visualise your encounter**

Example:

Sally Stands Up For Herself

While at work one day, Sally encountered a major problem with the company's computer network. The entire server had crashed and 23 employees had very little work they could go on with until the problem was fixed. This was a high-pressure situation, however she was doing her best to stay calm and she started to implement several testing procedures to help isolate the cause of the problem.

Sally's employer has always held her work in high regard, however he was not in the office on this particular day and Sally was under the direct supervision of the Office Manager, Judy. Judy is typically a disorganised person who is often late and behind in her work. Sally could sense Judy was becoming more and more tense as time went on and she made a few smart remarks suggesting Sally didn't know what she was doing.

Sally decided not to react to Judy's remarks because she had more important things to worry about. Sally's calm silence infuriated Judy even more until she snapped, "Oh for goodness sakes Sally this is ridiculous, you have been working on this for nearly an hour and we're all sitting here wasting precious work time. It's already 11:00am I was supposed to have the proposal to Bob half an hour ago and now you've made me look incompetent. Well you know who's incompetent around here, it's you Sally!"

The outburst had caught the attention of the entire staff. All eyes were on Sally. What would she say? What would she do?

Sally could hear her own heart thump in her chest and she felt the blood rush to her cheeks. Realising she was holding her breath she focussed her attention on breathing in through her nose and out through her nose. This helped to calm herself down so she could choose her words carefully. There were a million things she would have liked to say about Judy's work performance but she bit her tongue, knowing that replying with an insult would only make matters worse. What she really wanted was for Judy to leave her alone so she could focus on her job.

Sally spoke in a very calm and steady voice "Judy, what's important right now is for me to give my full attention to the problem with the server. I am feeling very distracted at the moment and would appreciate some quiet so that I can concentrate."

Judy huffed and puffed and walked away. A few people around the office sniggered at Judy. Sally was rattled but able to focus her attention back to her job.

Did you see how Sally handled the situation? She paused and paid attention to the emotion rising up inside of her. She focussed on her breathing to calm herself down. She refrained from entering into an aggressive slinging match about work performance. She kept her language 'I' focussed by owning the feeling of distraction and she identified what she wanted to achieve out of the situation—to be left alone. Of course this is just one out of millions of scenarios to discuss, however hopefully this helps to demonstrate how careful assertiveness can really help you in your everyday life.

However, it is important to recognise that being assertive doesn't always mean you will achieve your desired outcome. Sometimes it will not matter how calm and reasonable you are, you may have little success in altering another person's behaviour or point of view. In situations such as these, the most important aspect is that you have achieved your goal of being calmly assertive. Remind yourself of the Serenity Prayer and the wisdom behind knowing what you can change and what is best to accept and move on.

Dealing with Difficult People

It can be tough when you have to deal with difficult people, especially on an ongoing basis. However at some point we all come up against people who are just plain hard to handle and where no amount of calm assertiveness will alter their thorny reaction towards you or others around them.

Try to see these people as having a problem and as hard as it may seem, think compassionately about them. Have insight into what they may be going through themselves. They are potentially hurting, disturbed or under stress in some way and there is no need for you to get upset, angry or anxious when dealing with them. It really isn't worth your energy!

Instead, see the encounters as opportunities for you to grow. They will strengthen your resilience and coping skills that will benefit you throughout your lifetime. Think of the difficult person in your life as a chisel in the hands of a timber artist, and yourself as a piece of timber. The more that person carves away at you, the more beautiful and intricate you become as they help shape you into who you are.

Think of the difficult person in your life as a chisel in the hands of a timber artist and yourself as the piece of timber being carved into a beautiful work of art.

But perhaps a situation arises when you realise you were the person in the wrong. Or maybe you were overly focussed on yourself and did not take another person's feelings or circumstances into consideration? Perhaps it's time to apologise?

11. Apologising

A simple, well-formulated apology can go a long way. More than just a social formality, an apology is a fundamental way to demonstrate respect and empathy to someone who has been wronged. Sometimes it can be a critical factor in repairing or saving a relationship or your career, however its importance is often overlooked. If you are wrong or think you have upset someone, apologise. It doesn't need to be a long dramatic speech, but it should be sincere. If your apology lacks sincerity, it will also lack meaning to the other person.

A sincere, meaningful apology should include statements of regret, responsibility and remedy.

It's vital for your mental, and even physical, health to apologise for regrettable mistakes and misunderstandings. You will feel so much better for it. If you value the relationship with this person, apologising is important. The more important the relationship is to you, the more important it is to apologise. Ask yourself, is it worth loosing or damaging this relationship for the sake of making a point, maintaining your pride or just to be right?

Even if you know you are right, go gently. Just let the other person know why you think the way you do without being aggressive or smug. Simply agree to differ and move on with dignity and calmness. Remember, it is not about who is right or wrong, it is the one left cool and collected who triumphs in the end. Sometimes people later find out that they were wrong and may apologise to you!

These days there are so many different ways we can communicate and apologise to people. From face-to-face conversations, to phone, SMS, email and social media, there are lots of different communication methods to choose from. When apologising, consider what method would best suit the situation and the individual.

If the matter is serious and you send an SMS to apologise, chances are the other person will consider this to be a poor, insincere effort and become even more upset. Be brave, take a deep breath and apologise to their face, the results will often be well worth the effort.

If you find apologising difficult or scary and you do not know where to start, the following guide will help you to formulate a sincere, meaningful apology. Your primary objective is to communicate regret, responsibility and remedy.

Regret

Your apology should include a statement that explains your regret for causing the hurt or pain to the other person. While you may not have intended to harm anyone, you must acknowledge that you have done so and demonstrate your understanding of the damage you have caused.

Responsibility

You must take full responsibility for your actions. A meaningful apology does not mean making excuses to justify your actions or blaming someone or something else. Therefore a meaningful apology must include a statement of responsibility.

Remedy

You must demonstrate that you are willing to take action to remedy the situation as best you can. While no amount of apologising can undo actions in the past, the most important thing for you to focus on at this point is helping to mend the hurt you have caused. The best way to do this is to make a promise to take specific action that will ensure you will not repeat the behaviour. As the old saying goes, actions speak louder than words.

12. Public Speaking

While many people may not be required give slide show presentations in their day-to-day lives, we all come across situations where we have to speak to people in a formal setting such as during a job interview or when meeting your partner's family for the first time.

Speaking to a group of people is a terrifying experience for many, so how can you possibly relax and be yourself with all of those people watching you? Well it is easier than you think and we are about to teach you how. The added bonus is this will greatly help your broader social skills as well. Let's get started.

Be aware of your self-berating voice and pay attention to the tasks and thoughts that HELP you deliver your speech.

First of all, plan your speech, mentally rehearse it and visualise your delivery. By planning ahead and organising your content, you will have fewer worries clouding your mind when it comes time to deliver. The mental rehearsal and visualisation is just like practicing so when the time comes, you will feel experienced and calm because you have 'done' this so many times before. You can even pretend you are presenting your speech to your best friend or family in your living room at home. Speak as though you are speaking to them.

Be aware of the self-berating voice within. You know the one...I'm never going to get this right; I'm fat; everyone will laugh at me... Do not indulge in these thoughts, as they are extremely unhelpful. Instead, treat yourself kindly. Remind yourself why you are doing the speech and what benefits it will bring. Align your focus with the present activity and pay attention to the tasks and thoughts that help you deliver your speech. If you notice negative self-talk starting to unsettle you, stop what you are doing and ask yourself 'does this thought help me?' Chances are it will not, so put the thought down and refocus your attention.

Remember your Stick of Judgement. It is quite likely that the people you are presenting to are not on your judgement list so don't give your attention to worrying thoughts about what they might be thinking. Take the stick back off them and put it in your pocket. You are not concerned with their opinion because it does not matter to you. If the fear of judgement arises again that's okay, just keep taking the stick back, you are in full control; it will help you to stay calm and focussed.

Next, remember to breathe. In all seriousness, focus on your breathing and draw deep belly breaths, filling your lungs with sweet, fresh air. This will help you to speak clearly and present in a calm and relaxed manner. It is not a race to the finish line, so make sure your audience can understand what you are saying by projecting your voice to the back of the room and enunciating your words clearly.

During your speech, focus your attention solely on the task at hand, which is delivering information clearly. Focus on the meaning of the information and keep your mind in the external world. If you are using any form of technology to assist in delivering your speech, ensure you test your equipment before you begin so that nothing distracts you from your delivery.

Finally, pay attention to your body language. Make eye contact with your audience and be friendly. Don't fidget with your hair or clothing and ensure your posture is strong and straight.

So just to recap, here are the key points to remember:

- **Plan**
- **Treat yourself kindly**
- **Stick of judgement**
- **Breathe**
- **Focus on task**
- **Body language**

The great thing about these steps is that you can take these core principles and use them in your social life. For example, you might want to ask someone out on a date but just the thought of it is so scary that you have never done anything about it. Why not break the task down into these six steps, add in some of your new conversation skills and see how easy it can become to head out and have fun.

And remember it is how you approach the task of asking someone on a date that really matters, not so much the outcome. If you felt you did well through all of these steps but they declined the offer, that's okay. Don't fall into the trap of believing you are rejectable or a failure. Remind yourself that you did the asking well and that you are not in control of the other person's reaction.

The same goes for public speaking, you are not in control of your audience, they are a collection of individuals who will think what they want to think. The most important thing is to stick to your key points and rest will follow.

13. Self Image

Body image plays a significant role in how we feel about ourselves. Some people pay too much attention to it; others could perhaps take more care of their health and appearance. Either way, we would like to help you achieve a healthy, balanced and realistic perspective of your body.

Think back to the caveman mind. One of our primal instincts is to compare ourselves to others to avoid being rejected by the group. So in a way, it's natural for us to compare our appearance with those around us.

If you pay too much attention to social comparisons, you may experience strong feelings of insecurity and vulnerability.

The problem in the modern world is that we are constantly bombarded with airbrushed images of super models and celebrities from all over the world and our minds start comparing us to the wrong people. Is it any wonder we often feel less than adequate!

The first step towards a better relationship with your appearance is to accept that not everyone can look like a super model or a movie star. There is little point in comparing yourself to celebrities, as it will likely be the fastest way for you to feel miserable about yourself. Acceptance is the key here, remind yourself of the Serenity Prayer from chapter two and move on from the glitz of Hollywood.

We understand that social comparison doesn't begin and end with celebrities. We all have a tendency to compare ourselves to our friends, family members, colleagues, neighbours and even passers-by. Sometimes it just seems like everyone else is happier, sexier, wealthier and wiser than you, right? Well the problem is that you can not be envious and happy at the same time. It just doesn't work.

If you pay too much attention to the social comparisons playing over in your mind, you will no doubt experience strong feelings of insecurity, vulnerability and even helplessness. Instead, it is best for you to work towards accepting your perceived flaws and developing your strengths. Be authentic and embrace the fact that you are unique and no other person will ever be just like you, ever. Once you have reached this level of acceptance in your mind, you are ready to grow into being the very best you can be.

It's important to be realistic and to look after your body in a healthy and respectful way. There are serious consequences to your health if you get caught up in fad diets and over exercising, just as there are equal health concerns for carrying too much weight. Take action in areas of concern to you, but remember to do so in a healthy manner with the long term in mind.

Give your full attention to your inner beauty—your personality and mood. This no doubt sounds like a cliché, but if you are comfortable with yourself as you are, it will shine through for everyone to admire. People will enjoy being around a happy, interested person regardless of what you look like, rather than the beautiful person who is self-obsessed and complaining about their weight or appearance.

Pay attention to your posture and the expression on your face. Even if you would like to lose 10 kilograms, get your teeth straightened or buy a new outfit, by simply standing straight, smiling and making eye contact, you are well on your way to leaving a positive, lasting impression on those around you.

It's also important for you to be aware of body dysmorphia. This is where there is a disturbance in the way you perceive your body, caused by a distorted self-evaluation. For example, you may tell yourself over and over that you look a certain way and there is no convincing you otherwise, even if significant change has occurred. Some people take this to extremes and actually believe they are overweight when they are dangerously underweight. Don't trust your own judgement of your body image. If people keep telling you that you look great, believe them! They can't all be wrong and it is more likely you are in denial and holding onto a distorted image of yourself.

It's actually very common for older people to look back on photos and realise how good they really did look when they were younger. They are seeing themselves through different eyes; their perspective has changed. They often have a lot of regret about the struggle they put themselves through about their body image. Instead of relaxing and loving their body, which was beautiful as it was, they put all of their energy into hating the way they looked. The key cause of this is non-acceptance. Learn from their mistakes—enjoy the present time, you have it only once.

It's through the power of the present moment that you can really start to connect with yourself and the people around you. Take time to slow down and appreciate the fortunate aspects of your appearance. Instead of investing energy into wishing you looked a certain way and continually struggling with your image, you will get a much larger return on your investment if you focus on being the best you can be right now, with what you have. Again this might sound like a cliché; however the results will speak for themselves.

14. Value Yourself

YOU are your most precious asset and deserve ongoing personal maintenance just like your house or car.

Once you have persevered with your new way of thinking and defined who you are, you can't put your feet up on the table and think job well done. No, you need maintenance!

It is just like when you purchase a car or a house. You work hard, save up and make sacrifices until you achieve your goal. But it doesn't end there. The car needs to be serviced and the house needs to be cleaned. They both need a variety of ongoing maintenance so you can enjoy them in their prime and preserve their value.

You are no different. You deserve the same amount of respect (if not more!) and should perceive yourself as an asset that requires ongoing maintenance. By maintenance we don't just mean for your body, but for your mind as well.

There will come a time when a crisis arises in your life. You may completely forget about the Stick of Judgement and your mindfulness techniques. That is okay, it's likely this will happen, but the important thing is to become aware of this when it does happen and gently bring your attention back to some of the key strategies you have learned in this book. It may take time for these strategies to become second nature, but stick with it. Like learning any new skill, the more you practice the better you will become.

Sleep improves your mood, vitality and concentration levels so you can be fresh and at your best.

Health and Well Being

Sleep

It is very common for people to associate diet and exercise with health and well being, however there is a third component that many people neglect—sleep. It's vital to your health, performance and overall levels of happiness yet most people do not get enough sleep.

Sleep provides an opportunity for your body and mind to recover, rejuvenate and recharge so you are fresh and ready to take on the day ahead. It improves your mood and sharpens your concentration levels. When you are tired everything becomes a chore, you may become irritable with others or make mistakes at work. This in turn can effect how you think about yourself and you may beat yourself up about your general performance.

A good night's sleep (about eight hours) can give you a clear mind and a calm mood to help you navigate your way through your day. Most people say they don't have enough time to sleep more, they are simply too busy. This is the main reason why lack of sleep has become an epidemic. However, we all have the same amount of hours in the day; some people simply value sleep more than others. And it is not just about valuing sleep; it's about valuing the benefits of sleep, such as improved health, happiness and performance. It is about valuing you so you can be at your best!

We challenge you to pay attention to the amount of sleep you are getting each week and take action to improve it, if needed. You will be surprised how alive you will feel after just two weeks of consistently sleeping eight hours per night. But of course don't stop there—maintain it!

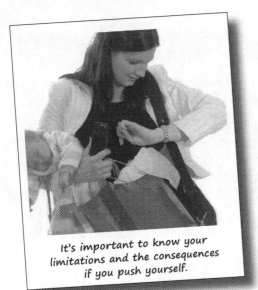

It's important to know your limitations and the consequences if you push yourself.

Learn To Say No

Many people lead extremely busy lives. Between work, children and social commitments, is it any wonder the years seem to fly by with increasing pace. Sometimes you can fall into the rhythm of attending every social event to which you are invited, or performing every favour asked of you.

While there are many benefits to being helpful and you may enjoy spending time with friends, there comes a time when you have to put yourself first. It's important to know your limitations and the consequences if you push yourself too far. If you are tired and busy, you need to rest. Refrain from accepting too many invitations or responsibilities; you do not need to say yes to everything all the time. People will still like you; they will not think less of you, especially if you are honest and upfront about why you are declining. Decent people will respect you for it.

Saying yes to everything can be a tough habit to break. Maybe you don't want to hurt someone's feelings or to miss out on some fun, so you go along even though you would much rather be doing something else. Your own needs and desires get pushed to the bottom of the list and everyone else gets bumped up to first place. Sound familiar? Consistently putting others first is not a sustainable way to live.

If you are really finding it difficult to put yourself first at times, approach it as though you are protecting yourself as a small child. You need to be kind and strong to protect the little you. You have needs, including rest, and you would make sure it happened for the little you, right? So you need to make sure you take care of yourself right now so that the little child inside of you is nurtured and protected.

Finding the Balance

The art to life is finding the balance in all of this! You need to find your own happy medium between being selfless and being selfish. We refer to the middle ground as self-respect. If you are a selfless people-pleaser and say yes to everything all the time, you run the risk of burning out. If you do not consider anyone else and never lend a helping hand, you will be considered selfish and people may lose respect for you.

To live your life somewhere in the middle you must remember to have a healthy amount of concern not only for others,

Find balance in your life by living with self-respect while having a healthy amount of concern for others.

but also for yourself and most importantly, for your values. By looking after your own needs first, you are better equipped to help others around you. Think about the safety demonstration presented by the air stewards on a commercial flight. In case of a loss of cabin air pressure, oxygen masks will drop from the ceiling to help everyone breathe. Airlines all over the world instruct passengers to fit their own mask first before helping others, including children! We are talking about exactly the same principle in your everyday life.

What good are you to others if you don't first help yourself? Think about the people in your life who depend upon you. Are you a parent, a wife, a husband, a boss, a friend, a neighbour, a sister, a brother, a colleague, a son or a daughter? There are people out there who care about you and the more you look after yourself and practice some self respect in your life, the more these people will enjoy your company. Plus you will begin to feel better about yourself and feel more confident with who you are.

15. Be Yourself Hypnosis

Our powerful customised hypnosis session will help you to feel more comfortable and confident with simply being yourself.

One of the things we find unfortunate about a lot of personal development books out there, is that you read them, learn all this great stuff, put down the book and forget about it. It is not hard to fall into this trap, but we want to make sure this doesn't happen to you after reading *How To Be Yourself*. In fact we are so passionate about making sure you implement positive change in your thinking and in your life we have created a customised *Be Yourself* hypnosis session as a gift for you. Your complimentary copy can be downloaded as an MP3 file from our website along with an eBook version of our book. Visit www.howtobeyourself.com.au and click on eBook & MP3, click add to cart and enter the following coupon code to redeem your free copy: F8176H9Z6. The hypnosis is split into two tracks, for your first time only, please listen to Track 01 because it explains important details regarding hypnotherapy. Afterwards, please feel free to skip Track 01 and start listening to Track 02 straight away.

The hypnosis will become an integral part of your own personal maintenance program where you can enjoy the benefits of professionally guided hypnosis from the comfort and convenience of your own home.

We understand that not everyone is familiar with hypnosis and that there is a popular misconception that hypnosis is some kind of unconscious state where you are unaware of your actions. You have all seen the stage shows right? People walk around like chickens and generally make fools of themselves. Well, they are just that—stage shows. They are not true representations of hypnotherapy but unfortunately that is the most common understanding people have. When under professionally guided therapeutic hypnosis you will not do anything you do not want to do, you are in full control. Let us explain a little further.

What is Hypnosis and How Does it Work?

Hypnosis is a wakeful state of physical relaxation where your attention is focussed on the suggestions and instructions from the hypnotherapist. When under hypnosis, you become more susceptible to these suggestions than during traditional therapy or conversation. Put simply, it is like turning off your conscious mind so that helpful suggestions can get through to your subconscious mind and bring about the changes that you desire.

This absorbed state of relaxation and heightened mental focus typically results in you having little awareness of your surrounds for the period of the hypnosis. This doesn't mean you will not know where you are or what you are doing—it simply means your mind will be distracted from your environment for the duration of the session.

It is the content of the suggestions made during hypnosis that give you results and they change depending on what area of personal development you would like to focus on. For example, the suggestions could be tailored to help you to quit smoking or lose weight. However in our hypnosis, the suggestions have been specifically customised to help you be yourself!

Jane Briscoe has been a qualified hypnotherapist since 1994 and experiences measurable success when using hypnotherapy in her psychology private practice in Australia. Jane has a Diploma of Clinical Hypnotherapy and is a Full Member of the Australian Society of Hypnosis (ASH). The Society trains only medical practitioners, dentists and psychologists in the field of clinical hypnosis and full members are those who have completed the society's training program and examinations. Jane's qualifications, experience and ongoing training with ASH are a testament to her competence and expertise in clinical hypnosis.

Jane has written and recorded this hypnosis session to further help you to:

- **Embrace your personality style**
- **Focus on your strengths**
- **Live by your values**
- **Overcome your fear of judgement**
- **Disconnect from unhelpful thoughts**
- **Advance your mindfulness skills**
- **Strengthen your interaction skills**
- **Live with self-respect**

Listening to the *Be Yourself* hypnosis in conjunction with reading *How To Be Yourself* will help to concrete all that you've learned throughout the book into your subconscious mind. The tools and techniques will become so ingrained in your thinking that they will become second nature to you and they will flow more easily into your everyday life.

For best results we recommend you listen to the hypnosis no less than twice per week and no more than once per day. As well as developing your personal thinking skills and confidence levels, listening to the *Be Yourself* hypnosis on a regular basis will also deliver the health benefits associated with regular, deep relaxation.

Hypnosis is safe, easy and effective, but using hypnosis alone without practicing any other practical techniques may not deliver major results. Remember that hypnosis is only one part of your maintenance program. Jane always stresses to her clients that hypnosis will not miraculously change everything on its own. You still have to implement change into your everyday thinking for the hypnosis to have a positive effect on your everyday life.

To get started, look at your weekly schedule and dedicate about half an hour twice per week purely for your hypnosis—purely for you! And don't forget to weave in some other personal maintenance such as getting more sleep, saying no to an unwanted social invitation or actively using your Stick of Judgement. Using the hypnosis in conjunction with taking action in targeted areas of your life will help you to achieve noticeable change in the way you think and feel about yourself.

16. Take Action

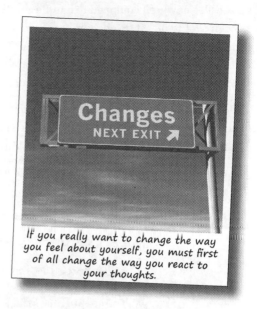

If you really want to change the way you feel about yourself, you must first of all change the way you react to your thoughts.

Congratulations on making it this far! It demonstrates that you are dedicated to living a more relaxed and happy life. Remember the key to being yourself lies with you. We have not waved a magical wand through the words in this book to automatically transform you. Rewarding and measurable change will require a little action from you from time to time.

Did you complete the personality style exercises in chapter three? If not, now is the perfect time to go back and do them, just reading and thinking about it will have nowhere near as much impact. It is time to embrace your personality style!

Did you complete the Brief Strengths Test and write down your top five with matching activities? If not, we really encourage you to do so. The online test is an easy multiple-choice format and only takes about 15 minutes to complete. Identifying and using your signature strengths will be one of the most important lessons you will learn from this book. Visit www.authentichappiness.org to take the test now!

Have you completed your list of people who can hold your Stick of Judgement? Have you practiced using it in real life? Keep this strategy in the top of your mind in your day-to-day life and you will be surprised how often you catch yourself giving your Stick to the wrong people. It is so refreshing and empowering to snatch it back!

Have you practiced a mindfulness exercise yet? Try to build one into your morning routine, like when you take a shower, walk the dog or travel to work. It really is the perfect meditation for busy people and it is as refreshing for your mind as a restart is for your computer. Like learning any new skill, the more you practice the better you become, and the more rewarding it is. Practice every day!

What did you learn about making conversation and interacting with others? Next time you are at a function or meet someone new, think back to some of the techniques we offered in chapter eight. Most importantly remember to ask questions, listen to the answer and focus on the present moment. Go back and re-read that chapter if you have forgotten some of the key points, it really is worthwhile!

You are also now well equipped to handle conflicts, apologies and public speaking. There has been a lot to digest throughout this book so don't feel flustered if you can't quite recall all of the details. Just keep *How To Be Yourself* as a reference book that you can go to when you get stuck or simply whenever you feel like it. In time, the specific techniques will come to you naturally and your confidence will grow.

Of course don't forget to listen to the *Be Yourself* hypnosis on a regular basis. Set aside at least half an hour this week to get started. The hypnosis is the easiest and most effective way to ingrain this new way of thinking into your everyday life.

And when a tricky situation arises in your life, remember how the instant emotional cleanse helps you to:

 Step 1. Clear away messy, unhelpful thoughts

 Step 2. Relax and calm your mind

 Step 3. Think more confidently

As we mentioned at the very start of this book, you can mix and match whichever techniques work best for you and build them into your very own, customised emotional cleanse. You might use your Stick of Judgement to clear away unhelpful thoughts, a mindfulness exercise to relax and refocus your mind, which therefore creates opportunities for more helpful and confident thoughts to arise. Whatever works best for you!

Remember, feelings and emotions are nothing but a direct result of the attention you give to your thoughts. If you really want to bring about positive change to the way you feel about yourself, we urge you to practice our techniques that help you to disconnect from unhelpful thoughts and focus on the present moment. However, please don't beat up on yourself if you have trouble remembering or implementing all of these new ideas. Thinking like that is unhelpful! Even if you take away just one new way of thinking after reading this book, then it has been worthwhile.

Perhaps you will simply be more aware of your thoughts and how they affect your mood and the way you feel about yourself? Awareness is a particularly powerful thinking skill.

Once you are aware of your fears and insecurities you are in a stronger position to make changes to your thinking patterns, bit by bit.

Or maybe it is your fear of judgement that really gets you down and the one thing you will take from this book is your Stick of Judgement and your powerful list of allies. Whatever new idea you enjoyed the most is the best place for you to start.

As you master this one new way of thinking, you will create more room in your mind for some of the other ideas to help shape your thinking, when you are ready. Slowly but surely, these thinking strategies will strengthen your social and emotional intelligence and improve upon the relationship you have with yourself. Some would argue this is the most important relationship of all. So come on, embrace your personal maintenance program and look forward to becoming a more confident and relaxed YOU!

Stay focussed on the present moment and persevere. And don't forget our advice about seeking one-on-one help from a suitably qualified health care professional if you are experiencing severe depressed moods and/or anxiety. We especially recommend therapists who practice Acceptance and Commitment Therapy, Positive Psychology, Mindfulness and Hypnotherapy. These are all of the therapy models you have just experienced by reading this book. We sincerely hope you enjoyed it.

Best wishes,
Jane and Simone

References

While Jane Briscoe utilises many of the ideas and techniques featured in *How To Be Yourself* in her psychology practice, we would like to acknowledge the following sources for their insight and inspiration. We also recommend these titles as further reading for your own personal development.

Listed alphabetically:

Engel, B. (2002), 'I'm Sorry: How Both Givers and Receivers of Apologies Benefit', Psychology Today

Harris, R. (2007), 'The Happiness Trap'

Hayes, S. with Smith, S. (2005), 'Get Out of Your Mind and Into Your Life'

Lyubomirsky, S. (2007), 'The How Of Happiness'

Seligman, M. (2002), 'Authentic Happiness'

Sharp, T. (2007), 'The Happiness Handbook'